VENICE
THE CITY AT A GLANCE

C000060591

Chiesa del Redentore
Andrea Palladio's church comes t[...]
during the Festa del Redentore in [...]
a wooden bridge is built across th[...]
Fondamenta San Giacomo

Chiesa di San Giorgio dei Greci
The Greek community was an important
presence in Renaissance Venice and this
Orthodox church, with its leaning belltower,
was founded in the mid-16th century.
Campo San Zaccaria

Basilica di Santa Maria della Salute
Baldassare Longhena's stunning basilica was
built in thanks after the city survived the 1630
plague, which killed one in three residents.
Fondamenta Dogana alla Salute 140

Palazzo Ducale
The former residence of the doge, and home
of Venice's council, law courts and prison, is a
mix of Gothic exteriors and classical interiors.
Piazza San Marco

Campanile di San Marco
One of the city's most iconic edifices, the
San Marco belltower is, at 99m, the highest
structure in Venice. It was rebuilt in 1912.
Piazza San Marco

Basilica di San Marco
Venice's enthralling cathedral is a unique
and exotic monument with a world-famous
facade, domes and mosaics.
Piazza San Marco

Molino Stucky Hilton
This striking 1895 flour mill and granary
had 1,500 employees in its heyday. It opened
as a hotel in 2007 after 52 years of closure.
Giudecca 810, T 041 272 3311

INTRODUCTION
THE CHANGING FACE OF THE URBAN SCENE

Venice is, of course, eternally beguiling and unique. But more than this, the city is a near miracle; its marble-clad palazzi built atop nests of wooden piles and soft mud. It also has a dwindling, ageing population and is notoriously resistant to change. When La Fenice opera house (Campo San Fantin 1965, T 041 786 511) burnt down for the second time in 1996, it was rebuilt to look exactly the same, which many see as indicative of the city's inherent provincialism. Yet the new millennium did bring in some rumblings of change. Renzo Piano worked his Midas touch on the Fondazione Vedova's Magazzini del Sale (see p037), as did Philippe Starck with his modern assault on Venice's hotel scene, Palazzina G (see p020). Equally impressive is Jacques Garcia's reworking of Hotel Danieli (see p026) and its rooftop restaurant (see p044).

Art foundations have received particular attention. Michele De Lucchi turned Benedictine dormitories into the art history library Nuova Manica Lunga (see p068) and Tadao Ando reclaimed the Renaissance Punta della Dogana (Fondamenta della Dogana alla Salute 2, T 041 271 9031) to house François Pinault's enviable art collection. In addition, Fondazione Prada is slowly restoring the baroque Ca' Corner della Regina (see p038), once an abandoned palace, into a contemporary art space. Even the cemetery on Isola di San Michele hasn't escaped the trend for transformation, with an extension by David Chipperfield due for completion in 2016.

ESSENTIAL INFO

FACTS, FIGURES AND USEFUL ADDRESSES

TOURIST OFFICE
APT della Provincia di Venezia
Palazzetto Carmagnani
San Marco 2637
T 041 529 8711
www.turismovenezia.it

TRANSPORT
Airport waterboat service
Alilaguna
T 041 240 1701
www.alilaguna.it
Travel card
A 72-hour travel card costs €35 and
covers both land and water services
www.actv.it
Water taxis (24-hour)
Consorzio Motoscafi Venezia
T 041 522 2303
www.motoscafivenezia.it

EMERGENCY SERVICES
Ambulance
T 118
Fire
T 115
Police
T 113
24-hour pharmacy
Check the rota displayed in all pharmacies

CONSULATES
British Consulate
Via San Paolo 7
Milan
T 02 723 001
www.gov.uk/government/world/italy
US Consulate
Via Principe Amedeo 2-10
Milan
T 02 290 351
milan.usconsulate.gov

POSTAL SERVICES
Post office
Salizada del Fontego dei Tedeschi 5554
T 041 240 4149
Shipping
SDA Express Courier
T 06 665 921
www.sda.it

BOOKS
Death in Venice by Thomas Mann (Vintage)
Venice: The City and its Architecture
by Richard Goy (Phaidon Press)
Venice Revealed: An Intimate Portrait
by Paolo Barbaro (Souvenir Press)

WEBSITES
Art
www.gallerieaccademia.org
www.guggenheim-venice.it
www.palazzograssi.it
Newspaper
www.gazzettino.it

EVENTS
Venice Biennale
www.labiennale.org
Venice Design Week
www.designweek.it

COST OF LIVING
**Taxi from Marco Polo Airport
to city centre**
€78
Cappuccino
€1.50
Packet of cigarettes
€6
Daily newspaper
€1
Bottle of champagne
€63

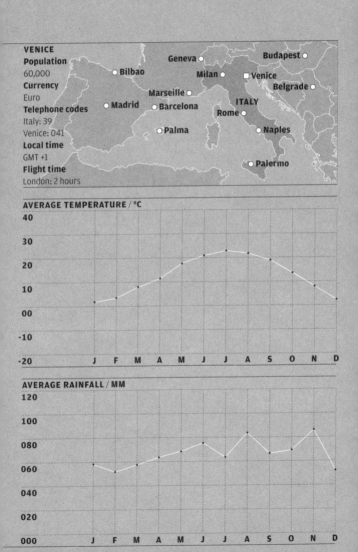

VENICE
Population
60,000
Currency
Euro
Telephone codes
Italy: 39
Venice: 041
Local time
GMT +1
Flight time
London: 2 hours

Geneva

Budapest

Bilbao

Milan

Venice

Belgrade

Marseille

Madrid

Barcelona

ITALY

Rome

Palma

Naples

Palermo

AVERAGE TEMPERATURE / °C

40												
30												
20												
10												
00												
-10												
-20	J	F	M	A	M	J	J	A	S	O	N	D

AVERAGE RAINFALL / MM

120												
100												
080												
060												
040												
020												
000	J	F	M	A	M	J	J	A	S	O	N	D

NEIGHBOURHOODS

THE AREAS YOU NEED TO KNOW AND WHY

To help you navigate the city, we've chosen the most interesting districts (see below and the map inside the back cover) and colour-coded our featured venues, according to their location; those venues that are outside these areas are not coloured.

CANNAREGIO

One of the city's six *sestieri* (districts), this area runs from the train station (see p066) almost to Ponte di Rialto (see p034). Although it contains the tacky Strada Nova, much of Cannaregio is quiet and pleasantly ruminative. The old Jewish ghetto is here, as is the Fondamenta Nuove, from where you can take a boat to the pretty Isola di San Michele cemetery and the islands of Murano and Mazzorbo (see p097) beyond.

GIUDECCA

Lying just south of Venice proper, this long, thin island has a different feel from the rest of Venice. Historically one of the city's poorest neighbourhoods, it has undergone much gentrification. The transformation of its huge 19th-century flour mill into the Molino Stucky Hilton (see p016 and p094) has helped. Giudecca is also home to the grande dame of luxury Venetian hotels, the sybaritic Cipriani (see p030), and Bauers Palladio Spa (see p089).

SANTA CROCE/SAN POLO

This is where you'll find the Rialto market (see p034), and the nightlife hub located around Campo Cesare Battisti. There are lots of bars and restaurants here, such as Vecio Fritolin (Calle della Regina 2262, T 041 522 2881), many with late opening hours and enviable views of the Grand Canal. Some of Venice's most significant artworks are housed at the Santa Maria Gloriosa dei Frari (Campo dei Frari 3072).

CASTELLO

Dominated by the Arsenale (see p014), formerly a military and shipbuilding powerhouse, Castello is the largest *sestiere* in Venice. Although now largely derelict, the Arsenale is partly used by the Biennales, the city council and private companies. The Art Biennale's main venue (Giardini della Biennale, T 041 521 8711) is just east of the Arsenale in public gardens inaugurated in 1895, housing 30 pavilions.

DORSODURO

To the south of the city, this zone stretches from the docks and working-class Santa Marta to the well-heeled streets around the Salute (Campo della Salute, T 041 274 3928) and old customs house (Fondamenta Dogana alla Salute). View Renaissance and modern art at Gallerie dell'Accademia (Campo della Carità 1050, T 041 520 0345) and Magazzini del Sale (see p037). Campo Santa Margherita buzzes until the wee hours. Stay at Centurion Palace (see p028).

SAN MARCO

The heart of the city, San Marco has the highest density of attractions – mostly packed into the great square (see p032) and church that give this *sestiere* its name – and high-end shops (see p072). Hotels Palazzina G (see p024) and The Gritti Palace (see p017) have both been given elegant makeovers. End your day here with an Aperol spritz at the Venetian institution Caffè Florian (see p041).

LANDMARKS
THE SHAPE OF THE CITY SKYLINE

Even if you've never even been to Venice, you will have seen the many domes of <u>Basilica di San Marco</u> (Piazza San Marco), as well as the intricate stonework of Ponte di Rialto (see p034), in scores of films and paintings. Such iconic renditions – Thomas Mann's multilayered *Death in Venice* and Nicolas Roeg's haunting *Don't Look Now*, for example – perfectly capture the intoxicating beauty and aura of this enchanting city built on water. Wandering through its labyrinth of *calle* (alleys), you could easily be transported back to a time when merchants and doges ruled the city. The tourist maelstrom surrounding Rialto, Piazza San Marco and the main thoroughfares connecting them to the station may jolt you from your reverie, but take the crowds in your stride and keep exploring.

Today, the city seems to exist on two parallel planes – one inhabited by fewer than 60,000 remaining Venetians and the other inundated with an endless wave of visitors. So you adjust. You get up early when the streets are empty. You see the city the way that the locals do – on foot – avoiding the crowded *vaporetti* and San Marco during the day. Above all, investigate each of the six *sestieri*, in particular the less-trodden Castello district in the east and Santa Croce in the centre. You'll probably emerge in a *campo* (square) teeming with children playing, adults gossiping and an almighty Romanesque church. That is the real magic of Venice.
For full addresses, see Resources.

Fondaco dei Turchi

Finished in 1227 by an exile from Pesaro, this palace was considered so beautiful that, in 1381, it was bought by the Venetian Republic and used for visiting dignitaries. In 1621 it was leased to Turkish merchants, who used it as a warehouse and residence, even installing a mosque (which was most likely the first in Western Europe) and a hammam. After falling into a dismal state of disrepair, it suffered an unhistorical restoration in the 19th century and was almost entirely reconstructed. Its striking pink-and-white marble facade was partly preserved, and its water-level arcade, first-floor loggia and distinctive round arches remain an awe-inspiring example of the Venetian Byzantine style. Inside is the Museum of Natural History. *Salizada del Fontego dei Turchi 1730, T 041 275 0206, www.msn.visitmuve.it*

Torre dell'Orologio

Piazza San Marco is not only home to the Basilica, Campanile and Palazzo Ducale but this beautiful clock tower as well, which you should take some time to admire. An incredible feat of mechanical precision, it indicates the phase of the moon and reigning sign of the zodiac, in addition to the time. In the past, it allowed seafarers to discern the most favourable hour to set out to sea. Commissioned by Doge Agostino Barbarigo more than 500 years ago, the tower was constructed by Giampaolo and Giancarlo Rainieri and inaugurated in 1499. In 1858, the clock was declared the official timekeeper of Venice, by which all other devices were set. Swiss watchmaker Piaget spent almost 10 years on its restoration, unveiling it in 2006. Tours are available by appointment. *Piazza San Marco, T 041 4273 0892*

Ca' d'Oro

One of Venice's most famous palazzi, the 15th-century Ca' d'Oro is where the family of Desdemona lives in Orson Welles' film version of *Othello*. This late Gothic palace was given the name Ca' d'Oro – House of Gold – in celebration of its ornate facade, covered in gilded carvings, ultramarine paint and varnished vermilion marble. The decorations have faded, but the exterior has survived essentially unscathed, its striking marble columns supporting exotic oriental arches. The interior has been modified by various owners and today houses the Giorgio Franchetti collection, dedicated to Venetian, Tuscan and Flemish painting, sculpture and tapestries. The most renowned artwork in the gallery is undoubtedly Mantegna's *Saint Sebastian*. *Calle Ca' d'Oro 3932, T 041 520 0345, www.cadoro.org*

Arsenale

Once the largest shipyard in the world, this imposing military complex is fronted by an elaborately decorated Renaissance gateway guarded by various classical statues and stone lions. Construction began in 1104, with continual extensions added from the 14th to the 16th centuries. During its busiest era, in the 16th century, its 16,000 *arsenalotti* could build a warship in just 12 hours. For a vivid description of the slaving workers, read Canto XXI of Dante's *Inferno* – the writer was inspired by his visits to the shipyard. Although part of the Arsenale is still used by the Italian military, shipbuilding was transferred to private yards more than a century ago. The rest of the building has been restored to provide exhibition and office space. If you visit during one of the Biennales, you should be able to get a glimpse inside.
Rio dell'Arsenale

HOTELS

WHERE TO STAY AND WHICH ROOMS TO BOOK

Venice's grandes dames hotels may never let go of the 18th-century decor, a formula of damask, gilt and Murano glass chandeliers. However, slowly and surely, some are daring to update, and a few of them have radically embraced contemporary design. High-luxe veterans such as Belmond Hotel Cipriani (see p030) continue to entice visitors, but the noughties brought about more modern options, such as the charming Novecento Boutique Hotel (Calle del Dose 2683, T 041 241 3765), and, in 2013, Aman introduced a resort and spa (see p018). That same year, The Gritti Palace (opposite), Hemingway's home in Venice, reopened following a restoration.

Over the past decade, hotels turning heads by breaking from tradition have included Palazzina G (see p020), now a showcase for Philippe Starck's interpretation of Venetian decor, and the Centurion Palace (see p028), relaunched after a modish interior redesign. Prior to this, the Molino Stucky Hilton (Giudecca 810, T 041 272 3311), set in a neo-Gothic former flour mill, injected new life into its quiet surroundings, whereas the reclaimed palace Ca'Sagredo (see p022) added grandeur to residential Cannaregio. The restaurant-cum-hotel trend also arrived in town. The Avogaria eaterie (Calle dell'Avogaria 1629, T 041 296 0491) is furnished with three elegant rooms, while neo-baroque nightclub 947 Club (Sestiere Castello 4337, T 390 477 3693) has four.
For full addresses and room rates, see Resources.

The Gritti Palace

This stately hotel launched in 2013, after a €35m, 15-month renovation to restore it to former glories. The Gothic palazzo has a rich history – built for the Pisani family in 1475, it became the private residence of the doge, Andrea Gritti, in 1525. It was first converted into a hotel in 1895, and now forms part of Starwood's Luxury Collection. Interiors, by Donghia Associates, combine antiques with modern pieces; the 61 rooms and 21 suites feature Venetian tapestries, Murano glass chandeliers, rococo couches and girandole mirrors, and the signature suites are inspired by famous figures who stayed here (Peggy Guggenheim, above). Outside, on the Gritti's terrace, you'll find the glamorous set busy taking in the many visual diversions of the Grand Canal. *Campo Santa Maria del Giglio 2467, T 041 794 611, www.thegrittipalace.com*

Aman Canal Grande
This first Italian venture from Aman has only 24 spacious rooms, but the rococo-style and neo-Renaissance living areas, like the Piano Nobile Lounge (pictured), cast a perfect frame for further repose. Private gardens, and keys instead of swipe cards, ensure that visits closely mirror the original palazzo experience. *Palazzo Papadopoli, Calle Tiepolo 1364, T 041 270 7333, www.amanresorts.com*

Palazzina G

Removed from busy Piazza San Marco, this 22-room boutique hotel, which opened in 2010, sits in an unassuming alley beside a wide bend of the Grand Canal. Fans of Philippe Starck will recognise the French designer's signature style, particularly his penchant for mirrors, more than 200 of which punctuate the interiors in various forms, as seen in the one-bedroom Grand Canal Suite (above). Spacious, modern and boasting some fantastic views, this is the best room in the house, amping up the glamour through its back-lit surfaces, white-on-white textiles and Fornasetti decorative accessories. Aristide Najean's modern Murano chandeliers and glass sculptures adorn both the lobby and PG's Restaurant & Bar (see p049).
Calle Grassi 3247, T 041 528 4644,
www.palazzinag.com

Ca Maria Adele

The most romantic hotel in all Venice, Ca Maria Adele launched in 2004. It quickly built up a loyal clientele, but refused to rest on its laurels, adding communal areas and a suite with a chromotherapy jacuzzi at the foot of its super-king bed. Choose between the subtle glamour of the five deluxe rooms, such as Room 119 (above), and two suites (339 has an extravagant terrace), or check into one of the five 'concept' rooms. La Sala Noire, for instance, is a sensual tonal blend of chocolate and aubergine, with a black chandelier. The Moroccan-inspired terrace, right next to the dome of Basilica di Santa Maria della Salute, is a fine spot for breakfast. In 2013, the owners opened a two-room hotel, Palazzetto 113, just next door. *Dorsoduro 111, T 041 520 3078, www.camariaadele.it*

Ca'Sagredo

This 15th-century palazzo is not just a hotel but also a national monument. As you climb the sweeping main staircase (opposite), which is flanked by marble cherubs and leads to the music room, admire the frescoes by Pietro Longhi and Giambattista Tiepolo and take on board the uniqueness of this property. Its original owner, Count Sagredo, was a man who was taken equally by pleasures of the flesh and the intellect; his library and bedroom – complete with a secret stairwell for his mistresses – have been respectively transformed into two Grand Canal Suites, Room 103 and the Historical Prestige Suite (above). Both are opulent, historic and intimate. The restaurant, L'Alcova, attracts in-the-know Venetians. *Campo Santa Sofia 4198, T 041 241 3111, www.casagredohotel.com*

Ca' Pisani Hotel
Venice's original designer hotel was
opened in 2000 by the Serandrei family,
who have owned Hotel Saturnia (T 041
520 8377) in San Marco since the early
20th century. This beautiful late 14th-
century merchant townhouse is filled with
1930s and 1940s furniture and art deco
design inspired by the futurist artists of
the 1920s. The hues are mustard yellow,
orange, beige and grey; the bathrooms
have hydromassage baths, and most
of the bedrooms – including the junior
suites (No 12, left) – feature a 1940s bed,
intricate woodwork, leather armchairs and
silver-leaf wardrobes and desks. Three
top-floor Deluxe Rooms offer stunning
views, a terrace, a Turkish bath, and a
shower for cooling off between cocktails.
*Rio Terrà António Foscarini 979a,
T 041 240 1411, www.capisanihotel.it*

Hotel Danieli

Built in the 14th century, for the city's powerful Dandolo family, Hotel Danieli is best known for its soaring three-storey Gothic lobby (opposite), an enduring architectural masterpiece and a local pick for coffee or cocktails. Four suites by French designer Pierre-Yves Rochon were unveiled in 2012, all of which have views of Bacino di San Marco. Three take their design cues from former guests Grace Kelly, Maria Callas and Greta Garbo (Signature Diva Suite, above), the starlets serving as muses for the marbled and mirrored interiors; the fourth is dedicated to the 12th-century doge Enrico Dandolo. Eight Dandolo suites were opened in 2013, also designed by Rochon. Piazza San Marco is just steps away, and a short walk to the north is the city's cultural hub, Fondazione Scientifica Querini Stampalia (see p064). *Riva degli Schiavoni 4196, T 041 522 6480, www.danielihotelvenice.com*

Centurion Palace
Don't be misled by the Centurion's neo-Gothic facade, set in Dorsoduro's quiet confines, for a veritable treasure trove of contemporary design awaits within. Architect Luciano Parenti worked on the historical restoration of the palace, and Guido Ciompi modernised the interior, creating 50 sleek rooms (405, pictured). *Dorsoduro 173, T 041 34 281, www.centurionpalacevenezia.com*

Belmond Hotel Cipriani

One of the lagoon's most fabled resorts, Cipriani epitomises Venetian luxury and opulence. Its location plays a part in this: the sprawling grounds, encompassing the 15th-century Palazzo Vendramin, is set at the tip of Giudecca and is accessible only by boat. In 2012, six junior suites were remodelled, each paved with pale grey travertine flooring with beige marble inlays. All have windows that peer out on to the hotel's herb gardens, the pool (opposite), or the lagoon, a vista also enjoyed from the lavish Palladio Suite (above). If you find some downtime, visit the Casanova Wellness Centre (see p088) or dine at the hotel's swank Cip's Club (see p039), Porticciolo Pool Restaurant, or the Oro Restaurant, which opened in 2014. *Giudecca 10, T 041 240 801, www.hotelcipriani.com*

24 HOURS

SEE THE BEST OF THE CITY IN JUST ONE DAY

Meandering around Venice's myriad canals and *calle* is delightful yet draining. Avoid the crowds by starting early, and take in the sights at Piazza San Marco – the overwhelming Basilica di San Marco, the views from the top of the Campanile, the pink-and-white Palazzo Ducale and its Bridge of Sighs.

Fuel up with a cappuccino and *cornetto* (opposite), then head to Rialto market (see p034) for some local fare. Devotees of the Renaissance should see the restored Chiesa di San Sebastiano (see p036), generally considered to be painter Paolo Veronese's Sistine Chapel. If your tastes are more modern, visit Punta della Dogana (Fondamenta della Dogana alla Salute 2, T 044 523 0313) or the Peggy Guggenheim Collection (Calle San Cristoforo 704, T 041 240 5411) and Magazzini del Sale (see p037). Even if you're not here for the art, architecture and film festivals, the Biennale foundation (www.labiennale.org) puts on events all year round.

You could easily ignore museums altogether and graze your way through Venice's culinary scene. For superb food and equally great views, reserve a table at Cip's Club (see p039). The city is noted for its snacks, so don't leave town without stopping in at one of its *bacari* (bars), like Cantina Do Mori (Sestiere San Paolo 429, T 041 522 5401), which serve drinks with small bites. After hours, make your way to the modish Caffè Centrale (see p060). *For full addresses, see Resources.*

09.00 Torrefazione Marchi

You'll know you're close to this popular café/bar before you arrive, as the heady smell of coffee pervades the surrounding neighbourhood. This roaster (one of just two left in town, and the only one that sells to the public) opened in 1930 and has changed little over the decades. The focus is on coffee, coffee and more coffee, a lot of it packed in jute bags piled high on the shop floor. And you know it's good because you'll be sharing the space with huddles of workers stopping for a caffeine fix, or housewives meeting to gossip. Try the *caffè della sposa* (made from eight of the best arabica blends) or a *Venexian* (coffee, cocoa and milk foam). Packets of beans, from Ethiopian Moka to Jamaica's Blue Mountain, are also available to buy. *Rio Terrà San Leonardo 1337, T 041 716 371, www.torrefazionemarchi.it*

10.30 Rialto market

From Monday to Saturday, at the north-western foot of Ponte di Rialto (above), this buzzy market is bursting with tasty produce from the nearby islands of Sant' Erasmo, Mazzorbo and Vignole – the origin of the products is often signalled by the word *nostrano* (ours). Stop for prosecco at Al Marcà (T 347 100 2583), a hole in the wall and one of the area's original bars, and sample *cicchetti* (small snacks) from local institution Cantina Do Mori (see p032). Choose from dishes such as tuna *polpette* (fishballs), marinated artichokes, *sarde in saor* (sweet-and-sour sardines and onions), bread topped with cheeses or *baccalà mantecato* (dry cod whipped into a creamy spread). Do as the Venetians do, and wash it all down with an *ombra*, a small glass of red or white wine. *Around Campo Cesare Battisti*

14.00 Chiesa di San Sebastiano

Most visitors to Venice head straight for the Basilica di San Marco, hence the frustrating logjam to get in. All the better for those who discover the city's other stunning churches, like San Sebastiano. Initially built to give thanks after a bout of plague, and reconsecrated in 1562, today it's a beautiful showcase of Renaissance painter Paolo Veronese's work, including his panels depicting episodes from the Book of Esther. You can also spot paintings by his contemporaries, Tintoretto and Titian. In 2012, the ceiling was completely restored, along with the facade, flooring and windows, thanks to Save Venice Inc, an American organisation devoted to conserving the city's art and architecture. Open Monday to Saturday, 10am to 5pm.

Campo San Sebastiano 1686,
T 041 275 0462

15.30 Magazzini del Sale

Reconstructed in 2010 by Renzo Piano, this 15th-century former salt warehouse on the banks of Canale della Giudecca continues the dialogue between the city of Venice and international contemporary art. Now an exhibition space more than 70m in length, it shows the work of Emilio Vedova among others. Attached to a rail along the ceiling are robotic shuttles that retrieve large works from the foundation's archives. This technology, set against a backdrop of cleaned and restored brick walls and beams, creates a stark visual dichotomy that at times diverts attention away from the art it contains. Buy tickets from nearby Spazio Vedova (Fondamenta Zattere 50), the Fondazione Vedova's second gallery. Closed Tuesdays. *Fondamenta Zattere 266, T 041 526 2626, www.fondazionevedova.org*

17.00 Ca' Corner della Regina

The enormous halls of this 18th-century baroque palazzo, designed for the former queen of Cyprus, Caterina Corner, are a riot of frescoes and Istrian marble. They're also now furnished with decidedly more modern embellishments, including works from Jeff Koons, Anish Kapoor and Charles Ray, courtesy of Fondazione Prada, which launched a contemporary art gallery here in 2011. The once-abandoned palazzo is under continual restoration thanks to donations by the foundation, which has a six-year lease; the restored rooms will open on a rolling basis through to 2017. Annual exhibitions are typically unveiled to coincide with the art and architecture Biennales, so check the opening hours on the website before you pay a visit. *Calle de Ca' Corner 2215, T 041 810 9161, www.fondazioneprada.org*

20.00 Cip's Club

On a summer's evening, getting a table at Cip's Club, located at the eastern end of Giudecca, can be the hardest thing to do in Venice. Part of the Belmond Hotel Cipriani (see p030), the restaurant not only serves some of the best market fish and produce, but enjoys arguably the finest views in the whole city, specifically the twinkling lights around Piazza San Marco. The terrace (above), an expansive wooden space fashioned after the deck of a yacht, sits next to a private mooring, where water taxis are stationed to shuttle visitors to and fro. The menu, which is full of seasonal specialities such as soft-shell crab on white polenta, or artichoke and potato soup with asiago cheese, is simple yet divine. Open from 7.30pm to 11pm. *Giudecca 10, T 041 240 8566, www.hotelcipriani.com*

URBAN LIFE
CAFÉS, RESTAURANTS, BARS AND NIGHTCLUBS

Take time to identify the particular culinary ways of Venetian life and the city gains another dimension. Although dining out in this town can be hit or miss, it helps when you throw caution to the wind. A snoop around Rialto market (see p034), specifically Campo dell'Erbaria and Campo Cesare Battisti – where a clutch of snack bars and restaurants serve excellent nibbles, pastas and grilled fish – is still the best place to start (and finish) your investigations. But even in the touristy San Marco district there are surprises.

Ristorante Terrazza Danieli (see p044), on the roof of Hotel Danieli (see p026), is excellent for a cocktail-hour snack or late-evening meal. Pizzeria Il Refolo (Campo San Giacomo dell'Orio 1459, T 041 524 0016) also has a marvellous terrace, as does the classic Ristorante Grand Canal (San Marco 1332, T 041 520 0211). Foodies on the hunt for a low-key gourmet meal should head to Mistrà (Calle Michelangelo 53, T 041 522 0743), or book a table at the mostly vegetarian osteria La Zucca (see p054). Old standbys such as Vecio Fritolin (Calle della Regina 2262, T 041 522 2881) are where Venetians still gather – always a good sign in a city rife with culinary flops. For *aperitivo*, there are fine views from Bancogiro (Campo San Giacometto 122, T 041 523 2061). After sundown, don your designer heels and dine at Muro (Campo Cesare Battisti già della Bella Vienna 222, T 041 241 2339).

For full addresses, see Resources.

Caffè Florian

Since opening in 1720, Caffè Florian has flourished as a Venetian institution thanks in part to the famous personalities who flock here for its coffee, unrivalled hot chocolate and sugary pastries. It doesn't hurt that the interiors are a set of gilded rooms, expanded and embellished by the Accademia di Belle Arti in the 1850s to include spaces such as the Senate Room, where the idea of the Venice Biennale was born. The café has entertained everyone from Casanova to Marcel Proust, and in warmer months the chairs and tables extend out on to the Piazza San Marco, where roving musicians perform classical numbers for the patrons. Florian continues to be popular, not only with tourists but Venetians and the cultural glitterati too. *Piazza San Marco 56-57, T 041 520 5641, www.caffeflorian.com*

Caffè Florian

Ristorante Terrazza Danieli

Few places to eat in Venice can match the views from this restaurant atop Hotel Danieli (see p026). In the warmer months, the terrace is flooded with sun, and the watery landscape, particularly the island of San Giorgio Maggiore, is unforgettable. Inside, a renovation by Jacques Garcia sectioned the room into cosy dining areas awash with seductive reds, greens, bronze and etched-glass mirrors that add depth.

The menu champions traditional Venetian cuisine, featuring dishes inspired by the lagoon's seasonal ingredients. Special olive oils are served with freshly baked bread, and waiters are well informed on wine pairings. We recommend the classics: *spaghetti alle vongole* with courgette flowers, and tiramisu for dessert.
Riva degli Schiavoni 4196, T 041 522 6480, www.terrazzadanieli.com

Aciugheta

Adjacent to the contemporary, stripped-back eaterie Il Ridotto (T 041 520 8280), is the equally pared-down and excellent Aciugheta; wooden beams and distressed brick walls are the extent of the decor here. This is not the place for heaps of Venetian seafood – instead, the focal point is the bar, its metal stools filling up at the end of the day with Venetians in search of *cicchetti* such as stuffed peppers or bread filled with cheese or anchovies, with a well-priced glass of house wine or a negroni. One of the main attractions of the restaurant is that, if you're after a quick lunch or dinner, the service is fast and the food is top quality. The pizza margherita with buffalo mozzarella and basil is probably the best in Castello.
Campo Santissimi Filippo e Giacomo,
T 041 522 4292, www.aciugheta-hotelrio.it

Harry's Bar

It is said that you haven't been to Venice until you've dropped into Harry's Bar. While it may be cramped and pricey, this legendary 1930s locale, now run by Arrigo Cipriani, son of founder Giuseppe, is a Venetian stalwart, with classically simple decor and a stylish ambience. A former haunt of Truman Capote, Orson Welles and, most famously, Ernest Hemingway, the venue still pulls in Hollywood stars and tourists alike, and it was declared a landmark by the Italian Ministry for Cultural Affairs in 2001. Order a bellini (the peach and prosecco cocktail that made Harry's famous) and then head upstairs to enjoy the spectacular views over the Grand Canal towards Basilica di Santa Maria della Salute (see p062). *Calle Vallaresso 1323, T 041 528 5777, www.cipriani.com*

PG's Restaurant

In a city where seafood is king, it's nice to find superbly rendered steak fillets and beef carpaccio on the menu. This modern take on a traditional lagoon restaurant combines the structure's original 19th-century columns with contemporary Murano glass vases and chandeliers, and mahogany furniture. Far from subtle, the decor can be a little overwhelming, which is where the Krug Lounge comes in, the first of its kind in Europe, to offer respite if it all gets too much. A small annexe beyond PG's dining area, this room brings a quietly sophisticated vibe by way of dark wood-panelled walls and plush brown leather sofas. There is also a small terrace overlooking the city's rooftops, stocked, of course, with plenty of chilled Krug. *Palazzina G, Calle Grassi 3247, T 041 528 4644, www.palazzinag.com*

Skyline Bar

The Molino Stucky Hilton (see p016) itself
may be enormous, unwieldy and perhaps
too standard issue for the discerning
design-savvy traveller, but its eighth-floor
Skyline Bar is worth the *vaporetto* ride. Go
at sunset and take your cocktails on to one
of the two terraces – either overlooking
Giudecca, with San Marco in the distance;
or out over the lagoon towards the smoky
skyline of the industrial town of Marghera
on the mainland. While you're up here,
check out the city's only rooftop pool (see
p094). Lunch can be ordered during the
summer months, and fare is mostly what
you might expect in Venice: light seafood
pastas and charcuterie plates. The bar
is usually busy from 7pm onwards with
a predominantly young and casual crowd,
and there's a resident DJ on Saturdays.
Closed Mondays from November to April.
Giudecca 810, T 041 272 3311,
www.molinostuckyhilton.com

Antinoo's Lounge & Restaurant

It's not often that white can be considered daring, but designer Guido Ciompi's stark minimal palette in Antinoo's main dining room (above) was a bold move in a city that favours swank ahead of subtle. The restaurant is located in the Centurion Palace hotel (see p028) and sits flush with the Grand Canal – it's awash with white tables and white leather chairs, and the circular relief pattern on the walls was inspired by shoals of fish. Regional seafood dishes dominate the menu, such as *tagliolini ai frutti di mare* (pasta topped with mussels and clams), and the staff are well versed in the provenance of the ingredients. Visit at sunset for an aperitif when the lounge is sleepy and you'll have better luck nabbing a table on the terrace.
Dorsoduro 173, T 041 34 281,
www.centurionpalacevenezia.com

La Zucca

This tiny restaurant is often heralded as
one of the only venues in town where
vegetables are equal, if not greater,
in status to fish and meat. Clad floor-to-
ceiling with strips of honey-coloured
wood, decoration is minimal. Order the
pumpkin flan and a glass from one of
the best wine collections in the city.
*Ponte del Megio 1762, T 041 524 1570,
www.lazucca.it*

Osteria di Santa Marina

Deservedly renowned for its elaborate cuisine and simple but effective twists on traditional Venetian dishes, Osteria di Santa Marina is quietly stylish, due to its wood-beam ceiling, polished darkwood bar, metal lampshades and windows overlooking a tranquil *campo*. During summer, it is possible to enjoy your meal in the restaurant's garden. The culinary delights include black barley risotto with puréed pumpkin and shrimp, and tiny grilled *calamaretti* served on a bed of potatoes fragranced with lime. Finish with a lemon and liquorice sorbet, and coffee with delicious homemade biscuits. Service is attentive, and the sommelier a mine of information. Closed for lunch on Sundays and Mondays.
Campo Santa Marina 5911, T 041 528 5239, www.osteriadisantamarina.com

De Pisis

Situated in one of the most enchanting spots in Venice, where the Grand Canal meets the Bacino di San Marco and the sound of moored gondolas bumping prows fills the air, De Pisis (above) specialises in rice dishes. The menu changes seasonally, so expect porcini mushroom and pumpkin risotto in autumn, and the simple, classic Venetian *risi e bisi* (a broth of rice and peas) in spring, although Japanese chef

Hiraki Masakazu has been known to sneak in the odd Asian flourish. After your meal, head to B Bar (in the same hotel), a cult nightspot in the 1970s, and now back in favour with the city's cool set. The 1950s vibe is achieved via gold walls, marble floors and a grand piano, and the sound system for DJ sets is a cut above.
Bauers L'Hotel, Campo San Moisè,
T 041 520 7022, www.bauervenezia.com

Osteria Enoteca San Marco
One venue to shake up the frequently
overpriced Venetian restaurant scene,
especially given its proximity to touristy
Piazza San Marco, is Osteria Enoteca
San Marco. Under dynamic management,
this revamped old-timer has exposed
brick walls, atmospheric lighting and a
glass counter filled with regional jams
and cheeses. The focus is on high-quality
spirits and wines, with some excellent
labels from Veneto and more than 400
varieties offered by the glass (bottles
and cases of wine adorn every nook and
cranny). The food is equally distinctive:
your John Dory might come lightly fried
in a crunchy sesame seed crust, or your
scampi served in a light spinach frittata.
Homemade desserts and pasta complete
what should be a memorable experience.
Calle Frezzeria 1610, T 041 528 5242,
www.osteriasanmarco.it

Caffè Centrale
This warehouse-style venue wouldn't be out of place in New York, but in Venice it's a one-off. You can eat and drink past midnight – order a *caipiroska alla fragola* (vodka, lime and strawberry) and sink into a divan. If you arrive by boat, one entrance opens directly on to a canal. You don't get more Venetian than that.
Piscina Frezzeria 1659, T 041 887 6642, www.caffecentralevenezia.com

INSIDER'S GUIDE
TOMMASO SPERETTA, PUBLISHER/EVENTS COORDINATOR

When he isn't organising art exhibitions and events, Tommaso Speretta can be found building the catalogue of his publishing company, Automatic Books (www.automaticbooks.org), at his Giudecca studio. He usually starts his day with a jog along the Zattere promenade, taking in Basilica di Santa Maria della Salute (Fondamenta Dogana alla Salute 140) and the Punta della Dogana (see p032). 'It's unusual for Venice, in that there are no worries about having to dribble between tourists,' he says of the route.

Speretta breaks up his workday with lunch at Cip's Club (see p039), where he orders the *sfogi in saor* (marinated and fried sweet-and-sour sole with pine nuts and raisins). Early finishes sometimes lead to cocktails at the Skyline Bar (see p050), or even a massage at Bauers Palladio Spa (see p089). However, a more typical post-work scenario is a visit to Al Bottegon (Fondamenta Nani 992, T 041 523 0034) for some *cicchetti*. At weekends, Speretta enjoys walking along the Arsenale (see p014) and stopping for drinks at Serra dei Giardini (Viale Giuseppe Garibaldi 1254, T 041 296 0360), before visiting an exhibition at photography gallery La Casa dei Tre Oci (Giudecca 43, T 041 241 2332). He doesn't shop in the city much but, when he does, cordwainer Gabriele Gmeiner (Campiello del Sol, T 338 896 2189) is his first stop. 'There are a few shoe artisans in Venice, but she is definitely the best,' he says. *For full addresses, see Resources.*

ARCHITOUR
A GUIDE TO VENICE'S ICONIC BUILDINGS

Venetians are adept at preserving and celebrating their dense and amazing Byzantine, Gothic, Renaissance and baroque heritage. Yet the city also has some less-beautiful 19th-century districts that could benefit from renovation. The 20th century, however, has given rise to several architectural gems: Casa Gardella alle Zattere (opposite) is a minor masterpiece, and Carlo Scarpa's interior for the former Olivetti Showroom (Piazza San Marco), along with his renovation of the 16th-century Fondazione Scientifica Querini Stampalia (Sestiere Castello 5252, T 041 271 1411) in the 1950s and 1960s, proved his mastery of different materials. However, Pier Luigi Nervi and Angelo Scattolin's 1963 Cassa di Risparmio (Campo Manin 4216) is thought anodyne rather than progressive.

Projects can be delayed for decades before they come to fruition, or are subsequently rejected. Of those that have been realised more recently, we would pick out Renzo Piano's Spazio Vedova (see p037), and the transformation of San Giorgio Maggiore's Benedictine dorms into cultural repository Nuova Manica Lunga (see p068). Santiago Calatrava's 2007 Ponte di Calatrava links Stazione Ferroviaria Santa Lucia (see p066) to the Piazzale Roma car park and bus terminal. Rem Koolhaas' revision of the Fondaco dei Tedeschi (Salizada del Fontego dei Tedeschi 5346) signals a gathering momentum towards a new architectural era.

For full addresses, see Resources.

Casa Gardella alle Zattere

Ignazio Gardella's marvellous L-shaped building – a modern version of a typical medieval Venetian courtyard house – was built between 1953 and 1958. The entrance connects to two separate groups of flats, one facing out to Giudecca and the other opening on to an interior garden. Both blocks are six storeys high and made with traditional materials such as the local travertine used for the bases and trims.

The window frames, balustrades, chimneys and doorways feature subtle references to 13th-century architectural ideas. Gardella was a great exponent of Italian rationalism, but he staunchly refused to be bound by its limitations. This building proved that modern Venetian architecture could be highly sensitive to its setting.
Fondamenta delle Zattere 401/
Calle dello Zucchero

Stazione Ferroviaria Santa Lucia

Venice's low-slung railway station is the gateway to the city. Some 82,000 people pass through daily (30 million a year) and for many this is one of the few modern buildings they'll see during their stay. The structure was the work of three architects over almost three decades. Chief engineer for the state railways company, Ferrovie dello Stato (FS), Angiolo Mazzoni worked on various designs in the 1920s before a competition awarded construction to the collaborative efforts of Mazzoni and Venetian Virgilio Vallot. Building began in 1936 and continued until 1943 but the station only gained its current appearance in 1950, when FS in-house engineer Paolo Perilli completed the job. The interior underwent further change in 2012 as part of Italy's ambitious Grandi Stazioni project. *Fondamenta Santa Lucia, T 041 785 670*

Nuova Manica Lunga

The Fondazione Giorgio Cini, the centre for Italian and humanist studies, based in a former Benedictine monastery, is a cultural treasure, where opera librettos, films and a collection of photography and academic archives are kept. In 2010, architect Michele De Lucchi converted the dormitories into a state-of-the-art library with 300,000 volumes for public use. White-pine tables and chairs, and the wood floors and bookshelves, look handsome against the wrought-iron balustrades and vaulted white ceiling. Banks of stainless-steel lighting fixtures have been installed above the shelves. Nuova Manica Lunga and its contemporary style have breathed new life into the island of San Giorgio Maggiore, a place that is becoming a hotbed of cultural activity and Biennale exhibition space. *Fondazione Giorgio Cini, Isola di San Giorgio Maggiore, T 041 271 0407, www.cini.it*

Former Saffa housing development
On the site of the former industrial area Saffa, these *case popolari* (social housing for low-income residents and the elderly) were designed by the Venetian studio Gregotti Associati. Construction began in 1981 on this complex, which features six low apartment blocks. Arranged around ersatz courtyards, it's crisscrossed by different sized paths (many lined with trees) that lead in and around the flats. Although the feeling is somewhat akin to wandering around a resort village, the homes do show thoughtful touches designed to make them blend in with the rest of the urban fabric. They have been painted an ochre colour that matches the bricks of neighbouring houses, and are lined with rooftop terraces similar to the *altane* that decorate old palazzi.
West of Canale di Cannaregio, between Rio della Crea and Calle Riello

SHOPPING
THE BEST RETAIL THERAPY AND WHAT TO BUY

It is a common misconception that the shopping in Venice is substandard; there is more on offer than cheap Venetian masks and fake Murano glass. If you have the time and patience, you can find original and tasteful local wares, including traditional crafts that have been produced in the city for centuries. After a visit to the Fondazione Scientifica Querini Stampalia (see p064), drop by the Querini Stampalia Bookshop (see p074) to find stunning blown-glass objects, handwoven fabrics and brilliantly forged jewellery. For papier-mâché Carnevale masks, the quality is high at Tragicomica (Calle dei Nomboli 2800, T 041 721 102). Other essentials include lush brocades, damasks and velvets, and paper.

Lace was a staple trade on the island of Burano but it is now mostly imported, although you can still find authentic pieces along Calle de la Canonica in San Marco. Another Venice-only experience is to be had at Atelier Segalin di Daniela Ghezzo (Calle dei Fuseri 4365, T 041 522 2115), where 18th-century replica shoes are crafted by the eponymous owner, the pupil of retired shoe-meister Rolando Segalin. For high-fashion, the major designer labels are located around San Marco, especially on Calle Larga XXII Marzo, Salizada San Moisè and Calle Vallaresso. While in the area, check out Bottega Veneta (Campo San Moisè 1461, T 041 520 5197), the luxury leather brand's second store in the city.
For full addresses, see Resources.

Attombri

This museum-like space is one of two showcases for jeweller brothers Stefano and Daniele Attombri, whose original store (T 041 521 2524) can be found in Rialto. The pair produce their elaborate, unique items of jewellery and objets d'art by hand, often incorporating antique Murano glass beads (they bought bags of tiny, historic *conterie* beads from a Murano factory when it closed down) and stunning alternatives of their own. Silvery nickel-free metal threads, which change colour with the light, strikingly encapsulate the city's relationship with the water. Fashion designers Romeo Gigli and Dolce & Gabbana are among the fans who have used the Attombris' pieces to accessorise their collections. *Calle Frezzeria 1179, T 041 241 1442, www.attombri.com*

Querini Stampalia Bookshop
A visit to the Fondazione Scientifica
Querini Stampalia would be incomplete
without a tour of the bookshop. Architect
Mario Botta carved out a space to house
contemporary art tomes and research
publications on exhibitions held here.
Also on display are objects by Italian
designers such as Afra and Tobia Scarpa.
*Santa Maria Formosa 5252, T 041 523
4411, www.querinistampalia.it*

Antonia Miletto

This small, sparse, orange-themed shop is filled with subtle jewellery designed by Antonia Miletto and made by skilled artisans in Milan and Florence. Miletto studied gems and architecture, and this is reflected in her jewellery designs. Her pieces are sold in New York, but this is her only store in Venice, showcasing a unique range of spiralling gold bracelets and diamond-studded ebony rings. Many of the designs combine exotic woods (cocobolo, macassar and purple heart) with semi-precious and precious stones (amethyst, diamonds, mother-of-pearl and turquoise). Miletto was among the first to experiment with the tough plastic methacrylic resin, and her collection incorporates this in a number of items.
Calle delle Botteghe 3127-3128,
T 041 520 5177, www.antoniamiletto.com

Studio Mirabilia

This veritable Aladdin's cave of weird and wonderful creations is the realm of Gigi Bon, an artist whose bronze rhinoceroses, two-headed lions and surreal paintings pay homage to Venice's sacred symbols. Look out for the likes of a rhino with the Basilica di San Marco etched into its side, or one sporting a comb-shaped *ferro* (the iron ornament at the front of a gondola), instead of horns and a nose. One corner is occupied by Bon's work table, where she executes her smaller sculptures, another by an open cupboard that is filled with shells, skulls and other exotic paraphernalia. Don't be put off if all this sounds too bohemian, go anyway, you'll be won over by Studio Mirabilia's charm. Open by appointment only, so plan ahead.
Calle Malipiero 3084, T 041 523 9570, www.gigibonvenezia.com

Caigo da Mar
Susanna and Riccardo Cargnel opened
Caigo da Mar in 2010 on an alleyway near
Campo Santo Stefano. This charming
boutique, where curios and various
homewares are beautifully appointed,
reflects their time spent travelling the
world collecting handmade objects.
Susanna, who often works in the shop,
is a font of information about designers
and Venice, and a joy to meet. Stock
includes John Derian curios paperweights and
plates displayed atop antique tables; Piero
Fornasetti furniture, incense holders and
perfume bottles bearing whimsical prints;
and porcelain artworks, plates and candle
holders with lace crochet imprints. The
shop also sells wool, linen, tweed, velvet
and silk cushions and pillows, oddities
such as stuffed animals and dozens of
candles by heritage brand Cire Trudon.
*Calle delle Botteghe 3131, T 041 243 3238,
www.caigodamar.com*

VizioVirtù
You could be forgiven for thinking you had
died and gone to chocolate heaven in this
shrine to the cocoa bean. City chocolatier
Mariangela Penzo has mastered and
modernised this centuries-old Venetian
tradition, coming up with such unusual
delights as ganaches laced with Barolo
Chinato wine, tobacco or balsamic vinegar;
dragées filled with ginger or coffee beans;
and chocolates made with that staple of
Venetian cuisine, pumpkin. There is also
a cocoa-rich array of spreads, *semifreddo*
desserts and mousses. On a chilly day,
pop in for a mug of spicy hot chocolate;
in summer, you'll find the iced chocolate
drink surprisingly refreshing. If you miss
the fix once you get home, you can order
most of the handmade products online.
Calle del Campaniel 2898a, T 041 275 0149,
www.viziovirtu.com

Massimo Micheluzzi

This Dorsoduro gallery/studio near the Gallerie dell'Accademia is the place to come for Murano glassware with a twist. Venetian-born Massimo Micheluzzi took an indirect route into design, studying history of architecture before working in the family antiques business, specialising in glass. It was after getting involved with the production of designs by Laura de Santillana (Paolo Venini's granddaughter), in 1990, that he became enamoured of the creative energy of the Murano furnaces. His take on this centuries-old tradition, in the form of collectable monochromatic vases and vessels, has a strong sculptural quality that displays a fusion of classic Murano techniques (*murrine*, deep-cutting and cold carving) paired with a real flair for contemporary design.
Calle della Toletta 1071, T 041 528 2190

L'Ottico Fabbricatore

Opened in 2012, this clothing boutique, selling ethically produced womenswear and accessories, is something of a secret in Venice. That might be because the store, owned and run by a husband-and-wife team – optician Francesco Lincetto and designer Marianna Leardini – is hidden through the back door of their lab. The low-ceilinged, white space is stocked with handmade Italian jewellery, silk blouses, cashmere jumpers and organic cotton dresses, alongside luxury eyewear and beautifully handcrafted purses and totes. Expect to find pieces by Faliero Sarti and Album di Famiglia, as well as sunglasses from L'Ottico Fabbricatore's own label and a selection of bags designed by Leardini. An area out the back shows the work of local artists and photographers.
Calle dell' Ovo 4773, T 393 335 9709

L'Ottico Fabbricatore

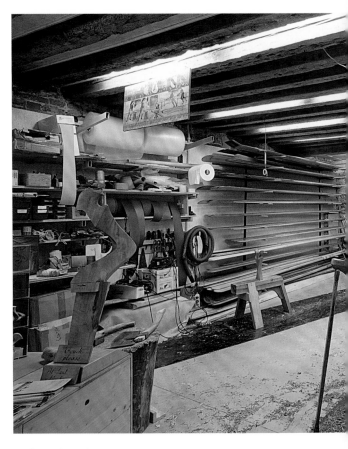

Le Fórcole di Saverio Pastor

In this workshop near Basilica di Santa Maria della Salute, Saverio Pastor hand-carves oars and *fórcole* (oar rests) for gondolas and other boats – he is one of only four remaining craftsmen in Venice, the only city in the world to vaunt this profession. *Fórcole* are made from walnut or cherrywood and each one takes an average of 20 hours to complete. Due to their complex lines, they're more akin to works of art, and there are examples at New York's Metropolitan Museum of Art and in the private collections of architects IM Pei and Frank Gehry. Pastor is savvy enough to realise that to stay afloat he must diversify, hence the scale models on sale to tourists, which are one of Venice's most beautiful and memorable souvenirs.
Fondamenta Soranzo 341, T 041 522 5699, www.forcole.com

SPORTS AND SPAS
WORK OUT, CHILL OUT OR JUST WATCH

Climbing Venice's many bridges and steps could be sport enough, but locals can't get enough of outdoor activities. Good places to jog include Fondamenta delle Zattere and Fondamenta della Salute in Dorsoduro, and most Venetians own a boat, in which they zip dangerously fast around the lagoon, especially in summer, when they flock to the beaches of Punta Sabbioni, Jesolo and Lido (see p090). Building up *una tintarella* (a tan) is a national obsession.

Even more popular are spectator sports; dozens of waterborne festivals happen throughout the year. Held on the first Sunday in September, the Regata Storica, a spectacular parade along the Grand Canal featuring typical 16th-century-style vessels and culminating in four races, dates back some 500 years. Even more impressive is the 30km Vogalonga race (www.vogalonga.it), held in late May or early June. Open to anyone with a rowing craft, it attracts more than 5,000 participants from around the world.

La Serenissima doesn't have a bevy of spas, but those on offer enjoy swank addresses at Giudecca's best hotels. Bauers Palladio Spa (opposite), which reopened in 2011, has divine products and a minimalist design. On the same island is the Molino Stucky Hilton (see p016), flaunting a 600 sq m facility comprising a state-of-the-art gym and a rooftop pool (see p094), and the Casanova Wellness Centre (T 041 520 7744) at the Belmond Hotel Cipriani (see p030). *For full addresses, see Resources.*

Bauers Palladio Spa

It might not be the city's biggest, but Bauers Palladio Spa, set in a convent-turned-hotel, has won more awards than any other in Venice. This spa occupies two floors and is separated into various treatment areas. One that stands out is the gold-and-green relaxation room (above), its one-way-mirror windows affording priceless views of San Marco. Eight perfumed treatment rooms offer such sensual delights as baths filled with milk and roses, and therapies utilising Himalayan salts and crystals. The location on Giudecca only adds to the restfulness, removed as the island is from the tourist thoroughfares of Venice. While you're being pampered, listen out for Elton John, who keeps a *pied-à-l'eau* next door.
Fondamenta delle Zitelle 33,
T 041 270 3806, www.palladiohotelspa.com

Lido beaches

Catch a ferry from Isola del Tronchetto, near Stazione Ferroviaria Santa Lucia (see p066), to Lido island, which is encircled by 12km of beaches. Although many of the public ones (*spiaggia libera*) leave a lot to be desired, you can have a taste of belle époque glamour in the bars and private beach clubs of Lido's stylish hotels, such as the early 20th-century Moorish-influenced Hotel Excelsior (see p096), with its luxurious thatched-roof beach huts. The ethereal atmosphere of Luchino Visconti's *Death in Venice* might be in short supply in third-millennium Lido, and the exhaust fumes shock after the car-free bliss of Venice, but a relaxing, sun-filled experience can still be had (at a cost), especially during the film festival, which runs for two weeks in September. *www.venicelido.it*

Bucintoro Rowing Club

Many of the local *cantieri* (boatyards) host rowing clubs partly funded by the city council in order to preserve Venetian traditions. These run lessons, sponsor regattas and hold social events. Founded in 1882, the Bucintoro Rowing Club is the oldest in Venice. It offers rowing (seated is known as *voga all'inglese*, whereas the Venetian style – standing up and facing forwards – is called *voga alla veneta*),

sailing and canoeing lessons and boat hire. Its Regata delle Befane (6 January) involves senior (aged 55 plus) male members racing from San Tomà to Rialto dressed as *La Befana*, a witch-type figure who, according to tradition, brings gifts to children who have been good during the year and coal (lumps of black sugar) to the naughty ones. *Punta della Dogana 15, T 041 520 5630, www.bucintoro.org*

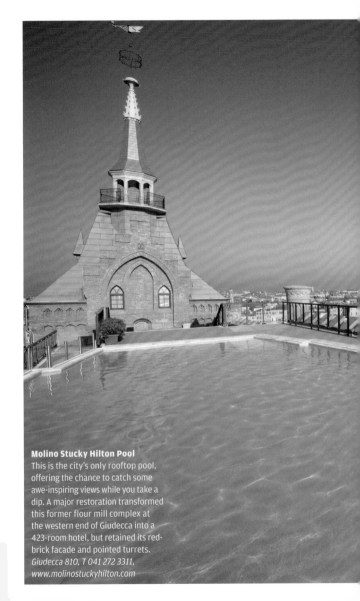

Molino Stucky Hilton Pool
This is the city's only rooftop pool,
offering the chance to catch some
awe-inspiring views while you take a
dip. A major restoration transformed
this former flour mill complex at
the western end of Giudecca into a
423-room hotel, but retained its red-
brick facade and pointed turrets.
*Giudecca 810, T 041 272 3311,
www.molinostuckyhilton.com*

ESCAPES

WHERE TO GO IF YOU WANT TO LEAVE TOWN

The highlight of a trip to the Veneto region is always Venice, but after a few days in this claustrophobic city, where getting around is an arduous process, you may need some respite from the crowds and the confusion. You can choose from a range of picturesque places, many less than an hour away, such as Mazzorbo, which is dotted with top-notch restaurants, including Venissa (opposite).

Treviso is pretty, and has good dining options, hip clothes stores and culinary festivals, including one dedicated to the *radicchio trevigiano*, a tasty local chicory. Asolo is a medieval town with stunning views and one of Italy's finest hotels, Villa Cipriani (Via Canova 298, T 042 352 3411), once owned by Robert Browning, while Padua is a lively university town. Vicenza was the home of 16th-century starchitect Andrea Palladio, who enriched the place with buildings such as the Teatro Olimpico (Piazza Matteotti 11, T 044 422 2800) and Villa La Rotonda (Via della Rotonda 45, T 049 879 1380). Ancient Verona offers a concentration of history and culture, and a Roman arena famous for its operatic spectaculars.

If it's a beach you're after, make your way to Lido island (see p090). To recreate Thomas Mann's heady *Death in Venice*, it's best to avoid the ungroomed public beaches and splash out on a cabin for the day. Book through one of the grand hotels, such as the Excelsior (Lungomare Guglielmo Marconi 41, T 041 526 0201). *For full addresses, see Resources.*

Venissa, Isola di Mazzorbo

The island of Mazzorbo, a 45-minute *vaporetto* ride from Fondamenta Nuove, is best known as a destination for walks along quiet canals, and long lunches at Michelin-starred Venissa. The restaurant is owned by the Treviso-based wine and prosecco maker, Bisol, which revived wine production on the island. Here, local fare is treated with reverence; vegetables, fish, fruit, cheese and wine are sourced directly from the surrounding estate and the lagoon area. Reservations for lunch or dinner are essential. Gianluca Bisol has also restored a nearby manor house on the estate, converting it into a boutique hotel, open from March to November. Its six airy suites, such as the Burano (overleaf), feature attractive wood floors and ceilings. *Fondamenta Santa Caterina 3, T 041 527 2281, www.venissa.it*

Salone degli Incanti, Trieste
This exhibition centre is known for its
focus on contemporary artists such as
Serse Roma ('Geometriche Dissolvenze',
pictured), a far cry from its previous,
less glamorous function as an indoor
fish-market. Architect Giorgio Polli used
neo-classical elements in the structure,
which was designed in 1913 to block out
the ugly dock buildings surrounding it.
Riva Nazario Sauro 1, T 040 322 6862

Museo Canova, Possagno

The small town of Possagno, situated amid the Asolan hills, features one of the most bizarre sights in the region – a huge 19th-century neoclassical temple. Designed by Antonio Canova, considered to be the last great Italian sculptor, it rises above the houses and offers brilliant views. Canova's family home, and two annexes built in the 1830s and 1957 respectively (the latter by Venetian architect Carlo Scarpa), now contain the Museo Canova, or Gipsoteca (right), one of the most appealing small museums in Europe. It hosts a comprehensive and memorable collection of Canova's work, including some of his lesser-known paintings and plaster models. The Scarpa wing shows the architect's skill in creating unexpected drama in a constrained space. Don't leave without a stroll in the lush gardens.
Via Canova 74, T 042 354 4323,
www.museocanova.it

NOTES
SKETCHES AND MEMOS

RESOURCES
CITY GUIDE DIRECTORY

HOTELS
ADDRESSES AND ROOM RATES

Aman Canal Grande 018
Room rates:
double, from €1,150
Palazzo Papadopoli
Calle Tiepolo 1364
T 041 270 7333
www.amanresorts.com

Avogaria 016
Room rates:
prices on request
Calle dell'Avogaria 1629
T 041 296 0491
www.avogaria.com

Belmond Hotel Cipriani 030
Room rates:
double, from €1,080;
Palladio Suite, €7,900
Giudecca 10
T 041 240 801
www.hotelcipriani.com

Ca Maria Adele 021
Room rates:
double, from €365;
Room 119, from €365;
La Sala Noire, from €520;
Suite 339, from €550
Dorsoduro 111
T 041 520 3078
www.camariaadele.it

Ca' Pisani Hotel 024
Room rates:
double, from €470;
Deluxe Room, from €540;
Junior Suite 12, from €660
Rio Terrà António Foscarini 979a
T 041 240 1411
www.capisanihotel.it

Ca'Sagredo 022
Room rates:
double, from €450;
Historical Prestige Suite, €2,530;
Grand Canal Suite 103, €2,750
Campo Santa Sofia 4198
T 041 241 3111
www.casagredohotel.com

Centurion Palace 028
Room rates:
double, from €290;
Room 405, €2,200
Dorsoduro 173
T 041 34 281
www.centurionpalacevenezia.com

Hotel Danieli 026
Room rates:
double, from €300;
Dandolo Suite, €960;
Signature Diva Suite, €6,000;
Doge Dandolo Royal Suite, €10,000
Riva degli Schiavoni 4196
T 041 522 6480
www.danielihotelvenice.com

Hotel Excelsior 096
Room rates:
double, from €200
Lungomare Guglielmo Marconi 41
Lido
T 041 526 0201
www.hotelexcelsiorvenezia.com

The Gritti Palace 017
Room rates:
double, from €1,150;
Peggy Guggenheim Suite, from €7,000
Campo Santa Maria del Giglio 2467
T 041 794 611
www.thegrittipalace.com

Molino Stucky Hilton 016
  Room rates:
  double, from €280
  Giudecca 810
  T 041 272 3311
  www.molinostuckyhilton.com
947 Club 016
  Room rates:
  prices on request
  Sestiere Castello 4337
  T 390 477 3693
  www.947club.com
Novecento Boutique Hotel 016
  Room rates:
  double, from €130
  Calle del Dose 2683
  T 041 241 3765
  www.novecento.biz
Palazzetto 113 021
  Room rates:
  double, from €380
  Dorsoduro 113
  T 041 520 3078
  www.palazzetto113.hotelinvenice.com
Palazzina G 020
  Room rates:
  double, from €350;
  Grand Canal Suite, €4,400
  Calle Grassi 3247
  T 041 528 4644
  www.palazzinag.com
Hotel Saturnia 025
  Room rates:
  double, from €155
  Calle Larga XXII Marzo 2398
  T 041 520 8377
  www.hotelsaturnia.it

Venissa 097
  Room rates:
  double, from €175;
  Burano Suite, from €245
  Fondamenta Santa Caterina 3
  Isola di Mazzorbo
  T 041 527 2281
  www.venissa.it
Hotel Villa Cipriani 096
  Room rates:
  double, from €195
  Via Canova 298
  Asolo
  T 042 352 3411
  www.villaciprianiasolo.com

WALLPAPER* CITY GUIDES

Executive Editor
Rachael Moloney

Editor
Ella Marshall

Authors
Rocky Casale
Giovanna Dunmall

Art Editor
Eriko Shimazaki
Original Design
Loran Stosskopf
Map Illustrator
Russell Bell

Photography Editor
Elisa Merlo
Assistant Photography Editor
Nabil Butt

Production Controller
Natalia Read

Chief Sub-Editor
Nick Mee
Sub-Editor
Farah Shafiq

Editorial Assistant
Emilee Jane Tombs

Intern
Gabriella Krichevsky

Wallpaper* ® is a
registered trademark
of IPC Media Limited

First published 2008
Revised and updated
2011, 2013 and 2014

© Phaidon Press Limited

All prices are correct at
the time of going to press,
but are subject to change.

Printed in China

Phaidon Press Limited
Regent's Wharf
All Saints Street
London N1 9PA

Phaidon Press Inc
65 Bleecker Street
New York, NY 10012

Phaidon® is a registered
trademark of Phaidon
Press Limited

www.phaidon.com

A CIP Catalogue record for
this book is available from
the British Library.

ISBN 978 0 7148 6906 3

PHOTOGRAPHERS

Sarah Quill/Alamy
Fondaco dei
Turchi, pp010-011
Torre dell'Orologio, p012

Fabio Amodeo
Salone degli Incanti,
pp100-101

Alessandra Bello
The Gritti Palace, p017
Aman Canal
Grande, pp018-019
Belmond Hotel
Cipriani, p030, p031
Ponte di Rialto, pp034-035
Cip's Club, p039
Caffè Florian,
p041, pp042-043
Antinoo's Lounge &
Restaurant, p052, p053
La Zucca, pp054-055
Tommaso Speretta, p063
Attombri, p073
Antonia Miletto, p076
VizioVirtù, pp080-081
L'Ottico Fabbricatore,
p083, pp084-085

Francesco Galifi
Venissa, p097, pp098-099

Attilio Maranzano
Ca' Corner della
Regina, p038

Elisa Merlo
Ca' d'Oro, p013

Francesco Radino
Former Saffa housing
development, pp070-071

Daniele Resini
Arsenale, pp014-015
Ca Maria Adele, p021
Ca'Sagredo, p022, p023
Ca' Pisani Hotel,
pp024-025
Torrefazione Marchi, p033
Harry's Bar, p048
Skyline Bar, pp050-051
Osteria di Santa
Marina, p056
De Pisis, p057
Osteria Enoteca San
Marco, pp058-059
Caffè Centrale, pp060-061
Casa Gardella alle
Zattere, p065
Stazione Ferroviaria Santa
Lucia, pp066-067
Studio Mirabilia, p077
Massimo Micheluzzi, p082
Le Fórcole di Saverio
Pastor, pp086-087

Lido beaches, pp090-091
Bucintoro Rowing
Club, pp092-093
Molino Stucky Hilton
Pool, pp094-095

Claudio Sabatino
Palazzina G, p020
Hotel Danieli, p027
Centurion Palace,
pp028-029
Magazzini del Sale, p037
Ristorante Terrazza
Danieli, p044, p045
Aciugheta, pp046-047
PG's Restaurant, p049
Nuova Manica
Lunga, pp068-069
Querini Stampalia
Bookshop, pp074-075
Caigo da Mar, pp078-079

Matthew Shaw
Hotel Danieli, p026

VENICE
A COLOUR-CODED GUIDE TO THE HOT 'HOODS

CANNAREGIO
Venice's main entry point, and a tranquil alternative to the more well-trodden *sestieri*

GIUDECCA
A historically rundown archipelago that has been attracting some serious investment

SANTA CROCE/SAN POLO
With hip bars, restaurants and the Rialto market, this central district is always bustling

CASTELLO
The Arsenale is where the big guns of art and design gather for the Venice Biennales

DORSODURO
Head here to visit world-renowned art collections in impressive architectural settings

SAN MARCO
La Serenissima at its most iconic – and home to some of the city's most desirable hotels

For a full description of each neighbourhood, see the Introduction.
Featured venues are colour-coded, according to the district in which they are located.